*Druthers*

*Flood Editions, Chicago*

# *Druthers*

JENNIFER MOXLEY

PUBLISHED BY FLOOD EDITIONS

WWW.FLOODEDITIONS.COM

ISBN 978-0-9981695-3-8

DESIGN AND COMPOSITION BY QUEMADURA

PRINTED ON ACID-FREE, RECYCLED PAPER

IN THE UNITED STATES OF AMERICA

# Contents

TO

ROBERT HERRICK

AND

SAM ''LIGHTNIN''' HOPKINS

WHO

SAVED ME

FROM DEEP BLUES

AND DARK WOODS

THESE *DRUTHERS*

ARE MOST HUMBLY

DEDICATED

# *Druthers*

# If a Lion Could Talk

It was only the dawn
of the Christian
movement, but Jerome
was already wise
to it—he knew
that but for a man
who is not a man
trapped inside books
would latter-day painters
lose their perspective
somewhere along
the vanishing point.

So he tied his body to a
great denial and scolded
his widow patron's daughter
for the crampy hungers
gathering in hers.

Leaving behind his
ascetic theater he let
his rags polish the floors
as he delighted in the
intercourse of a
little night reading.

The dog-faced lion
played along, shedding
the sweaty mane-cape,
rewarded each night
for his loyalty
with a bowl of kibble.

Jerome gazed out
of the casement
at a beautiful scene,
stars fanning the cool
expanse of lapis
desert dome,
and chuckled
to himself, "No one
paints a saint

in a great library
built through the pilfer
of a pious widow's gold."
A scholar, he knew
that sainthood, just like
good translation,
requires a bit of
finger pointing,
and some ethically
questionable
sleight of hand.

## Druthers

I would rather run a butter knife
Through Ruskin's uncut pages
Than under the lip of a stuck tack.

I would rather come under a hand
That's apt to undo me than be
Buttonholed by a walking dictionary.

## And the Angels Sing

The burden of heaven
grips me in your bite—
     it's not right
but what can I do? Your
grin plucks such unthink-
able melodies into being
my eardrum can hardly
take it. Tunes that build
sandcastle beauties in
my conch, straight out
of *Architectural Digest*.
I can't afford it, the angelic
judgment of your
distracting smile, without
being thrown out on
my heel, dazed by
trumpet-playing ninnies
in unisex robes who blow

on cue like Xavier Cugat
in *You Were Never Lovelier.*
I'm lost. One glint off
the white of your incisors
and I'm whisked inside
the celestial philharmonic,
deaf to all necessities
of this mortal slip.

## Well Enough

Alike the Mal Content and the Do Gooder
Must wrong illuminate to see their right,
While the curious soul, brightened by laughter,
Leaves right where it is, robbing wrong of light.

## The Eros Threshold, Coming and Going

*Spiritus mundanus*
   a midnight
      mist-veil
unwicked droplets creep, ignite,
   crackle
the length of this weighty cavern,
   a million subcutaneous pulsars
spark-turn
   inside the membrane,
      redraw
      the clock, hang it anew
in the expansive no place
   of atemporal
      syntax: *There is no place*
*like home.* I lost from my ear the seven strings
   in questing too long
      for the mother's kiss. It's
not, I thought, the One in the Many

but earthly memory and
even a trick. Now I turn and find
in your kiss
the true vector of wheres
unasked for. I make the pass,
enthralled by Eros exiting
just as when entering I was
moon-blind and night-seeking
over gravelly pavements and grass. Each other
tastes unlike each
other, outside the station
wagon muffled voices, smell of weed, hard flesh:
through matter to no matter to
ever and where.

# Blue Chirp

I'm dancing in a heated room,
Outside it's bitter cold,
   With Mallarmé blue above
   And Emerson white below.
Although I dance I am not young,
Neither am I old.
   My knees in plié creak,
   My breasts are feeling low.
Drenched in sweat and all a-fry
I crack the window just a bit.
   The arctic bites my skin,
   And then I hear a little tit,
A songster in the winter blue
Blurt out a happy tune.
   Bitter chill be damned,
   He *will* his lover woo!
A matchless mix of feeling!
A flute of Stéphane's *idéal,*

And draught of Waldo's
Here and now!
This moment trumps a thousandfold
Those chubby maiden days
Courting gloomy moodiness
Beneath Parisian gray.
And though I never tarried,
My rose was often plucked,
To tell it I was weary
No matter who I fucked.
But now I'm like that winter chirp
Defying all that's mean.
I kiss my Heurtebise awake
And blow him in my dreams.
Both Azure and Experience
Besprinkle me with dew
To make perpetual Maytime
In age burst forth anew.

# The Old Prick

No couplet does our love constrain
Nor leaden bow could snuff it out.
It's blind, some say, but bandaged so
   Delights in conversation.

We read in bed of Love's high name
In philosophic foldabout;
Our sheets have leaves, but also dew,
   And never sublimation.

Youth-skewed Cupid, the little pain
We banished just like Bradstreet's book,
Yet ere he went he lodged anew
   The arrow's deep affection.

Thus older Love feels much the same
As young love does, absent the doubt,
Instead of pain or *please don't go,*
   Sweet skill and satisfaction.

## *Elizabeth Arnold's* Life

"Envy is a sin, put it away,"
said the man in the elevator
clutching the keys to his room
with the better view.

But I can't help it,
I envy you.

I want a farm desk
and a shepherd friend.
I want to send my
soul to school.
I want to have thought up
the awkwardly satisfying
rhyme of "surprising"
and "crying." The tears
of trees, no less!

Have I grown impatient
with poetry, to take
such pleasure in another's pain?

The cleaving of the heart.
The loss of possible love.
A dream of the death of the sun.

Fellow poet, you've made
a sage study of the earth
and of the body's flow—yet still
I offer a small correction:

It wasn't the drugs talking—
the sun *is* a god. A god
of fire telling you to back
away from that volcano!

## My Fear

Not of dying but of finding myself
very much alive, but with nothing
to read. Like the old *Twilight Zone*
episode in which a zealous reader,
finally left alone with his books,
breaks his eyeglasses on the rocks.

Verne couldn't bear that Cyrus Smith,
Gédéon Spilett, Harbert, Pencroff,
and Nab had Top the dog, but not
one book to read on their
Mysterious Island and so he arranged
for a trunk to bring a few volumes ashore.
Crusoe had only the Bible
and the journal he himself kept.
"But they had the Book of Nature."

Once I may have been able to live
quite happily with only trees,

or so I thought when I read
about this kind of quaint and simple
life in a book written for girls.

But now I know I need those
scrapings left on pulp by my
own kind. Real physical books
that I can hold in my hand
and read by the light of the
blaring sun on my desert island
built for one. Please don't ask me
to play that parlor game and whittle
my list down to ten. I want what
Jerome had in the desert, a private
library full, well curated, and grand.

My fear is waking up to find myself
trapped in the present, online,
in a plane, on a bus, a hostage or a
houseguest, in prison cell, what have
you, without silence or a book,
where a screen of trite disturbing
news plays on continuous loop.

# Herrick in the A.M., against His Wishes

*In sober mornings, doe not thou reherse*
*The holy incantation of a verse*

It's best to keep still in a blizzard
they say, and I agree. The Christmas
lights need taking down, the cat's
asleep and so's the husband. The
electrician won't be stopping by,
and fingers crossed, we'll keep the heat.
How sweet to read of springtime
in poems about love and roses,
written near about the time
a king was to be killed. Outside
a swirl of milky dust sings a
bracing verse, heaps a blanket down.

## Happiness

Happiness, too clever by half,
For want of you I lost my gift
Along the thread of youthful noise
In search of favors from the boys.
Your harmony, most mysterious,
Spins silently through the universe,
Yet your secrets sound sweet music
For those who have ears to hear.
Alone and far from ceremony,
Empty dramas, all that's phony,
Aged out of the social game,
Happiness, you came my way again
And looked just like that child who
Disliked the cage of public school,
Big groups of kids, conforming all,
While from the canyons, insects call
Like your sweet rhyme, fashions be damned.

Such echoes most don't understand;
Latin declensions, wind-swept leaves,
A book, a cup, *these* are my loves.
Happiness, it kills me to see
You, my first love, come back to me.

# Sadness

Sadness, you are not to be missed,
Nor your sad eyes in darkness kissed,
And so I'm showing you the door.
Your library is far too poor:
It holds no words or lines divine
But only serves to dim the sign.
Nor is the sweet melancholy
Of contemplation's beauty
Your boon—you don't love rhyme,
Locked as you are in ego's tower
Fretting about things you cannot change.
You remind me of that girl who fled
The side of her dying mother's bed
To wander through all words confused,
Fabricating grand theatrics of self
Without the slightest clew or worth.
Sadness, you still come in mourning
And look just like the face of those

Whose eyes I'll never see and whose
Voices, so familiar, I'll hear no more.
Sadness, you break my heart, just like
A maudlin old-fashioned poet.
You're the great love of my adulthood,
But I would leave you, if I could.

## Article of Faith

I was made unwell
by knowing too well
what could not happen.
The sameness of
failures and surface
actors. Death, friend,
a promise of peace
across the fence.
Impoverishment
enriched. No more
double-folded life
where all is poisoned
by recollection,
cognizance of the
wheel, wrong pat-
terns. Night's descent
turned vision blind,
but dawn redeemed

by crystal sparkle,
mirror signal, savior
-line which my
dead eye fished
up to pine, in-
sight restored.

# The Closer

FOR FRED

Who knew what he knew,
none can say,
yet there was play—
an imagined hero—
in him, and in
some women—
tolerance, desire, love.

And alone, he was,
who knows?
Sweetness, an impulse,
fatigue
   beats me,
his loss
   keeps me
lost, back there

before he was
so long in stir—
locked up.

Now that he's
gone I can
no longer keep
what exists
(no longer)
at a distance.

# The Tenuous Here and Now

*The slim line*
*that leads back*
*to the wide way.*
KEN NORRIS

Their impatience had set the hands of the clock
back to the present void. Etymology clicked past,
yet still they flatly stared 'til finitude was all her sense
and her age awakened. She awoke in a dark place
and as if called to begin the poem she had long been
waiting for. Before her eyes a line began to draw itself
between the stars. Orion rebrightened. And then the stars
were eyes worldwide cast upward all throughout
this history (called human) and also much before.
Starbursts of light. Having so long predated her
the message was predicted and she welcomed into it—
as if what's called eternity had all the patience in the world.

The heavy curtain left her hand and she returned to bed,
tucked into the man that is "a sweet . . . marriage."
The finite poem, its small words, fell apart, parted, to particles,
into the atomic motion of the whole. Cat-like, her head curled,
pressed into the darkened paw of back, toward the steady warmth.
A whiff of bleach, the softness of a sueded T, old, white.
A whimper addressed to sleep, troubled.

Yet neither the static of impatience nor the terror
of visions could be stilled. The key of ancient stars
was hunter's bow and she was shot, unlocked, pushed
inside a dizzy cave of mind unending: her lover's
body but a fragile ledge on which, still breathing,
she tightened her selfish grip.

As a practitioner of half-peace she was not ready for the fall.
Addicted to longing and to language. But aren't these
words as sweet, said the lights? And didn't you see
some bright filament of forgotten mind
translated in the finite poem? She was legs and toes,
stretched out, cat-like, oblivion-seeking, happy.
Alone the poem can say it. In company all is lost. Why is this so?

The poem of the whole punctures through the mythic
fiction of the group. As social the code circles, denies or
polishes the feeling, the feeling passes unnoticed
outside the words of the poem, trapped in the
lie of that parrot language, called *impatience*, "Is *this* what
you want me to say?" No, not even *that*, the question,
but instinct, reaction—the tenuous here and now.

The reader has her dreams. They are not constructs
but bow-written wounds caused by the hunt, the
taste of a dirt-blood kiss, as if she'd crumpled bent-
kneed to the ground her memory its hungry lover
spasmodic sinews signaling the no-going-backness of
her loss. Having no language but that of the master
the dogs come after, shred what's left of her.

Had she seen Diana in Orion's arms? Or are hunter
and lover one? Bent-kneed to the ground to become part
of the whole, the hole parted the hands clasped,
palm on palm and darkness (they say) was revealed.
You must fall to pieces like the dreams of the penniless.

The impassioned moment killed the chronometer,
thought stepped down word histories, bright desires
coined and stilled quivered anew. A stellar music, soul-tuned.
Infinite this language, though the receptor, flesh portal
(called human) is not. Through its decay she was her mother,
her mother's mother and all the dead besides, through its
excitement she was all the hands she'd ever touched
or reached for, guided up here, pushed down there.
Her definition was infinite in the hands of the whole.

# The Miracle of the Stubborn Mules: A Valentine

Full stubborn the mother
who gave you life
and then gave you away.

Full stubborn the mother
who took you in
and then named you
after the Protomartyr:
poor stoned Steven,
left out in the desert
for the beasts to eat.

A brokered living thing,
translated from mother to
mother. A full stubborn
miraculous life. A life
as contested as a
Saint's relics, fragments

gathered and reburied:
A bit of bone lost,
a drop of blood found.

Recovered in Jerusalem,
it was hoped that Saint Steven's
remains be translated
to Constantinople, to be
housed in the Imperial Palace.

But they never made it.

When the coffin mules
reached the gates of the city
they refused to take another
step. It was God's will.
They even spoke it.

Those mules were as stubborn
as a surrendered baby
born in the coldest quarter
of the year, given an
interim name, passed
from hand to hand,

as stubborn as my love
for that foundling, who found
my heart and stubborned forth
a love there, a love that will
no more be moved
than divinely inspired mules.

# The Cradle

My consort is in concert with the waves.
He dolphins through the seaweed ropes, salted
With flesh-memory of his youthful days,
The purpose just existence, exalted
Body set free from calendared hours,
The ransomed life, the hourglass sandstorm.
To my consort it seems the sea authors
A form he must follow, he must perform
An ichthyan act: robbed of oxygen
That he might feel dissolved in that kindless
Edge of presence, which lives within the lexicon
Of ear—a breath-robbed tide-dandled blindness
In which my consort counts the beats, five-fold
Iambic "deaths" recoiled from ancient shore,
Five-fold the poet's dance to patterns old.
A radiation from the cosmic core
Attracts the man with whom my fate's attached,
His life-trace succumbs to the sea's deep rhyme
When up from primordial death he's snatched
By that rhythm moon-gripped, element sublime.

## Orbit Music

A creamy tear descended here when Cupid squeezed the teat
of Venus. Dripping down the Milky Way it puddled beneath
old oak, new pine. Love's selfish thirst did pluck a cosmic note,
set every entombed entangled bit of me in roots both new
and old to singing. I was become in earth and by harmony
a million bits of tongue and ear, sound funnels upwhorled
in song conducting cones. Fresh music from old flesh
corrected my (most melancholy) record of this last go round
the planet. Now I was first things: elementals, vegetable
and mineral in form, dust to kick it on the breeze,
loam to feed old oak, new pine, Eros-greedy energy
on hunt for nourishment, cream to suck, breast to squeeze.

*Sundries*

Waits there the book unread,
the sketch still hoping to be handed
its lead, brushed from inner eye
through digits onto pulp. A block
of index cards, Wheelock, and
a homemade chart of participles,
subjunctive uses, hang fire in a
canvas bag: with the patience
of the dead, Latin also waits.

Parted from these enumerated
hungers by the need to purchase
sundries: things hardly worth
their handle: to cleanse, soften,
perfume, and comfort the skin
I sit within, and from which—
though mental transports mark
the eye's pencil, trace the use
of words extinct—I cannot part.

# Appointment

One onus on an empty calendar
    Penciled in at three o'clock
Is more blood-tick to the soul's good humor
    Than a whole day eaten of work.

## The Teacher's Copy

Along the poem's right margin I find marks:
Revenant of an English Renaissance
Specialist I once knew. Ballpoint runnel,
Cursive crag of q, oblique T-square t's,
And curbside to quatrains the commentary:
*Wilt thou meet arms with man*, "from questioning,"
*For sure thy way is best,* "to acceptance
Of the human condition, unity
Of the cosmos." *Make one place ev'ry where.*
Notes to measure the poet's tempering
By God as second to secular test.
Yet, sieved through the holes of pocked abstraction,
The poem's self in feeling gathers withal
In the pure gesture of the teacher's scrawl.

## Wanted Attention

Miracle Gro crystals
blue the water
inside the watering can.
The thirsty houseplant
cranes toward
the new spring sun.

You open your
blue down vest,
invite me in. My
neck cranes up to find
a kiss that wants for
nothing, unfastens all.

## The Give and Take

I slap you back and curl into a shell
Because that heaven you take me to
Is also like a hell, the edge of which
I see whenever you take your leave
At sweet love's end and I, a muscle
Boneless, mollusk lacking shell,
Am once again bordered by tongueless
Thought: inimical dwelling, flanking
Fleshy intuitions of all-connectedness,
This arid chronometer is just wrong
Enough to tick down the pleasant throb.

# Variation on a Poem by Herrick

Love, I have broke
  Thy yolk;
What was clear-eyed
Upon the plate
  Is naught
But dismal smear.

My failed attempt
  To spear
My Love and oust
The ache instead
  Outspread
And now I'm toast.

## The Follow-through

Freud said that *interruptus* in *coitus*
Too often practiced can lead to madness.

Nor does Muse-brought ecstasy, once begun—
    Though different in kind—
        Abide frustration.
The repressed line break, the uncoupled rhyme
    Come back as madness
        In the poet's mind.

# Poet and Bureaucrat

Better a poet than a bureaucrat, the husband
says, desiringly. Though both need bureaus,
or is it beds, a bureau bed on wheels, rolled
out beside the writing desk of any bribable
bureaucratist, should the poet (it is unlikely)
prove to be a dish. Both bureaucrat and poet
suffer of corrections more than average and
both are piqued by piles, consternated hourly
by inefficient days of old, the human clunk
of cog-less systems for the bureaucrat to bear,
like to the clang of ornament from verses
much anthologized inside the poet's ear.

# Back to the Business of Being a Poet

Would-be bureaucrat no more. Will
The husband roister upon hearing the
New roster? The first order of business: clover.
Even though it's snowing. A roll around
On warm ground: greenest grass preferred,
But dirt will do. For desk a rock upon the chest
Just like skalds of old. Pastoral pleasures
Denied the bureaucrat sitting behind glass,
In front of screens, fingered, dusty. The idle
Bureaucrat looks busy, the busy poet, idle,
That's their business. Would the office
Be less sterile were the bureaucrat a poet?
Words do fly, but in the arid HVAC air
They're swatted and subsequently squashed
Beneath the plain soles of bureaucrats, even
Such with good intentions who spare the
Poet the business. What is a poet to do?

## Riddance

May the Muse see fit to rid me
Of my worldly capability.

How else avoid the perils of gifts
That lead elsewhere than laurels?

## On the Level

Around 1985 I began to project my future
into the 1920s, free of the corset, newly
enfranchised, a girl with a haircut like
one of the guys. In the future I would be
the heroine of a Vera Caspary mystery,
listless in my studio apartment littered
with stockings and cocktail shakers. I
could just see myself balancing cozily
on the pinstriped knee of my sugar daddy
while he sweated out multiple gin martinis.
"Gee doll, you're *swell.*" He winks at me.
And though I'm not actually very pretty,
he pulls my head back with a handful
of platinum and plants one on the collar.
Damned if I know why he gets to me.

In the years to come there would be other
pasts, but in 1985 it seemed to me that the

1920s had all I could ask for.
A New Woman bohemia before hippies
or yuppies (then called Babbitts, whom
everyone laughed at), with gold-tipped
cigarettes and Chanel No. 5. There weren't
any cell phones in my future, but just
down the hall from my apartment was
a phone for residents only. The faded
wallpaper added necessary melancholy,
geometric calla lilies, Art Deco motif.

In 1985 I thought the only screens
in my future would project moving
pictures of silent idols or be hung
nonchalantly with peach slips
and tap pants, a garter belt or two,
used to cordon off a dressing room
in the corner of my studio. Without
these dreams of the 1920s
how could I have pinned my hopes
on an adulthood of something
besides cash registers and classrooms?

My parents, having fled their pasts,
had no way to build a future. I had
the crackle of jazz-age recordings
preserved on 1980s vinyl. Listening
prepared me for 2015's haunting
by technological memory, but not
for its presentist static, those super-
abundant incremental distractions not
on the level with any future, or past.

## A Light Touch

Some would have it that women long to exit
All the mess of it, men pursuing, undressing
The breasts, the rear, the legs, a hand up
To the carriage, or gently down the back.
"This dance of care's a foot upon the neck,"
Some say. Yet I say the righteous clench trumps
Not the sigh, and so I'd miss it, by the by.

## The Bittersweet Echo

The junkyard kitten has the need
For the love-starved boy to bring it feed
On his way back home from school—
To correspond, to break the cool.

And rhymes are lullabies to mourning
And pretty the pain of human longing.

# The Poetry Lesson

J. Alfred Prufrock's pathetic "Love Song"
Remains a favorite with the young,
But when I recall my early years,
I preferred *The Flowers of Evil*—
A work of genius that confirmed my fears
That we're all susceptible to the devil:
Any red-eyed dandy in a redingote
Haunting Paris with a goatee gloat
And cloven hoof can come to seduce
The souls away from splenetic youth.

For such Goth verses I am still keen,
But more in the spirit of Halloween;
For serious things I turn, as in girlhood,
To songs of spring, and Christmas caroling,
To poems that don't prevent me seeing
That most men and women are good.

Prufrock's high-waters and tedious streets
Pale beside Herrick's puddings and meats,
But when Eliot labeled Herrick "minor"
He doomed us to his gloomy mirror,
Forgetting that, for better or worse,
Both with rhymes did bind their verse
(*who knew such sonic scrappiness*
*would lend itself to so much happiness?*).
And both stood for King and Country,
Though Herrick was fitted to his century
While Eliot, outdated, Herrick's envied.

## Druthers (2)

I would rather be convinced
To stupefaction by wine or gin
Than by a tedious conversation.

I would rather a dry white
Than a dry night, a teetotaler's flak
Than not hit the sack.

# Orison on a Dark April Morning

For my body I only hope
   To return to the birth
   Of our fair universe,
To that first music of the Bang—
   The whoosh of matter flung—
     In ear rehearse.

Its echo there has helped me cope
   With life's contingency
   And all I cannot see,
To sense the presence of quantum
   Logics, the stellar hum,
     Inside of me.

For my spirit I pray that dope
   Apollo quit his pout
   And tell these clouds to scoot.
Stop drinking whiskey, draw his six-
   Gun, and once and for all give
     This gloom the boot!

## The Chip

I was not yet not a girl, maybe eleven,
when my dad put his hand on my shoulder
and asked me to step off the court.
"We want to play 'a man's game,'" he said,
which he and my older brother then did.
How could he not want to play with me?
I sat on the concrete step
drenched in prepubescent sweat,
nursing the wounding exclusion.

Not long after I began to understand
that in my neighborhood most of the men
preferred other men to women.
I said some ugly things about them
in earshot of my mother.
How could they not want to play with me?
She smiled and talked me down.
Their choice is not against *you,* she said.

Neither, I now realize, was my dad's.
He had the right to enjoy
his competitive adult game.

For a long time I maneuvered
grand theoretical frames
to explain these petty exclusions,
preoccupied with my own defense.
But not every personal wound
is a world-historical offense.

My dad, a familiar stranger,
excluded me this once. Not long after,
with the help of a bullet
he excluded himself once
and for all. But not every personal sorrow
amounts to a world-historical disaster.

The lives of others are difficult to erase,
more difficult than we might think.
There's always a rock to contain them,
a fractured Styrofoam cup
stained with yesterday's coffee.

*I love you*, I wrote in dirt
the afternoon of the day he died. And I did.

Sometimes when walking I feel him,
like a great resentful snail weighted by
disappointment slowing down my steps.
The snail upsets my settled happiness
with thoughts of *I want*, of *why can't I have*,
of *so this is all I've managed to accomplish?*
I no longer mind this little part, nor the gift
of not being seen. The lack that makes me
look anew at all that's right before me.

I used to feel wounded by the money
he left me, robbed of his time and
company. I thought to have preferred
his hand on my shoulder inviting me back
into the game. What a fool I was.

## *Flutter Out*

This form, *content,*
this tear, *a rent*
that stills, *this shell*
that fears *and will*
not bear *the years.*
In wake *of death,*
this line (it's said)
elsewhere a care
will lead, a mind
direct—therefore
the soul, *a bow,*
a word *in stir*
inside *the mouth,*
inmate *for life,*
not sown *but wound*
unless *unleashed*
into the yard,

into that play
of deep content
between *two forms*,
where things *refuse*
as well do grow.

## A Bouquet Garni *for Rosmarie*

A sprig of *rosemary* bedded in a ribbed
Celery canoe, laurel leaf and thyme
To perfume Rosmarie's collages.
The vowels drift gently . . . in her name
The worker *E* won't come between
Decadent *S* and *M,* that we might
*Sm*ell the pepper of the poet's bite.
An answer she is, my Rosmarie,
No question—so *Y* folds in
And dots itself turning Romantic *I,*
That Rosmarie's pen might split it,
Bind, blend, and reclassify.

# Enigma Porter

FOR JR

before     aft

*à chercher*

a searcher

her     ear

as

text     mirror

*elle suit*

a belle suit

an able

suit     case

*avant*     *après*

the apt

threshold

the old trifold

tremble

*trésor* chest

60

*porté par l'énigme*

    porter

through the portal

 of fragmented

   defenses

  *défense d'entrer*

sleep    illness

memory  mortality

*mortalité  mémoire*

*maladie    sommeil*

   *interdit*

   interred dream

the instant   the vision

 the fluffy white tail

of the poem's swift body

   disappeared

(a trace    *à tracer*)

   into Dante's

    garden:

    GAME ON

    *jeu*

# Into the Penetralium: A Light
# Poem on a Dark Matter

Returning to an old book about a dark and brutish love
somewhere in gloomiest England, I stumbled upon you,
Penetralium, and you would not let me be. "Oh Jennifer,"
you said, "Why must your mind make me conjure alien
tentacles from sci-fi movies?" "Yes! That's it, poor Penetralium,
there you are stuck on John Hurt's face, sending a slimy
reproductive organ down his oral cavity!" (I *hate* the word
cavity). "Oh, Latinate friend, might I enjamb you?" Pene-
tralium . . . neurons sliding through my mental worm-
holes from outer space all the way back to Rome!
A dark moist cavern, like Bluebeard's castle in Bartok's
one-act symbolist opera . . . a fetish chamber from which
John Cowper Powys might hide his eyes but fill his mind.
"You are so soft and so hard, Penetralium!" "Jennifer,
before you go mad, for Christ's sake look me up!"
"But I want to flex my mind without reliance on
sources and guides. I've studied Latin, I know better.

Let's see . . . Pen-e-tra-li-um . . . your *um* ending
could be nominative or genitive. Are you second declension
or third? Is *pene* for five? Like the mysteries of the penta-
gram? Oh no, there's that *t,* so terribly Greek!
How about *pen* for penumbra? You are the threshold
of the darkest regions, O, might you be but a penetrated thing?"
I'm prisoned again inside muscled walls, clamping and oozing.
O powerful Isis set me free! Or how about you, OED?

## My Muse

My Muse, though intrepid, is very shy,
And won't come under watch of another's eye.
Unless he's bursting with unspent prose,
In which case, he's shameless, and anything goes.

# The Honest Cook's Insomnia

It's best to start with desire.
A vivid imagination of the end result
of your culinary efforts—
both the pleasure in the mouth
and the admiration of others—
is inevitable, but do not
overindulge in such fantasies
lest you undermine surprise
and set yourself up for disappointment.
Do not cook to impress
others or conform
to their tastes. Nevertheless
you should be as attentive
to the palate of who you are
cooking for as lovers are to the
whims of the beloved, so that
their desires become your pleasures.
The formal restrictions of
another's diet may be the expansion

of your own. Yet you cannot please
everyone. Choose wisely
when planning a dinner party.
Do not cook for people whose tastes
are wildly divergent from each other
or your own. Do not try to please
"the crowd." It is better to
risk accusations of exclusivity
and stay honest to your vision,
than to go hungry cooking for those
whose tastes you do not share.
Always strive for what M. F. K. Fisher
called "good honest food."
Do not cook in an emotional state.
Be passionate in the planning,
but clear-minded and deliberate
in the execution. A focused mind
need not preclude a last-minute
innovation: that sudden impulse
to add capers to your tomatoes
vinaigrette may make the dish.
Beware of trends and fashions,
yet open to new techniques.

Just because the food magazines
begin picturing plates piled high
in fetishistic columns, with no
regard for the integrity of meat,
starch, and veg, doesn't mean
you can't still "plate" like your
great-grandmother did. Let your
guests intermix forkfuls as they
please. But don't be perverse.
Just because something is popular
doesn't necessarily make it bad.
Topping salads, toasts, and pastas
with a cheery egg, fried or poached,
though *all the rage,* is irresistible
and inexpensive, a fashion that
channels our nostalgia for old diners
and "breakfast served all day."
Learn from the masters. This is true
for amateurs especially, so often
exiled to the flimsy techniques
of the present day. All cooks must
work to deserve their inheritance,
so the Rombauers knew when

they chose an epigraph from the
German Romantic poet Goethe
to open their famous *Joy of Cooking*:
"That which thy fathers have
bequeathed to thee, earn it anew
if thou wouldst possess it."
A solid bank of knowledge will
make up for temporary shortfalls.
You may end up in a kitchen
with old equipment, or with
only one knife to your name.
Let the restrictions of your material
conditions pressure your Muse
into new creations. If you lack
inspiration turn to the bookshelf.
The classics are bossy and know
their mind. "A dry hamburger
is not acceptable" (Marion Cunningham),
"Pour this over the fish and rush it
to the table. Not a dish to be kept
hanging around" ( Jane Grigson).
Imagine yourself at the table with them.
Don't be smug about outdated foods.

Remember, even iceberg lettuce
was once thought elegant. However
much of an innovator you imagine
yourself to be, your time's tastes will
express themselves through you,
and cooks who come after will
scratch their heads. The 1970s was
mad for Swiss-style cheese fondue,
the 1980s for Italy's sun-dried tomatoes,
such reaching after European dash
looks rather quaint against
the current mania for Asian fusion.
You will always feel nostalgic
for your first exposure to revelatory
flavors. Though you later realize
that your "discovery" was part
of a culture-wide *zeitgeist,*
your memory will grant you
authorship rights and a pat on
the back for your "innate" good taste.
Taste, like experience, feels individual
but is more often than not shared.
Food is culture. Eating or cooking

for health alone is like reading
bad political poetry, you may feel smug
while swallowing, but you'll go to bed
dissatisfied, with a fierce craving
for unhealthy snacks. Extreme diets
make sense only under doctor's orders,
as religious practice, or as bids
for attention. The honest
cook cooks to eat, not to gain
compliments or coax others into
stomaching meals they've no desire for.
If you ruin a meal, don't force yourself
or your diners to eat it. Admit
defeat, order a pizza, and move on.
The honest cook's insomnia will
rehearse the failure and find a solution.
There are bakers, and there are cooks.
I learned this from a writer friend.
Bakers are conceptualists, he said.
Everything is weighed and measured,
mixed and kneaded *before* heat is applied.
By the time the bread goes into
the oven the creative act is over.

The ingredients and conditions (high
altitude) control the outcome while
the baker passively waits to see if the
end result is successful. A cook prefers
the ever-evolving field of the fry pan.
The sizzle of aromatics, the tossed-in
vegetables, the sear of fat. A pinch of this,
a dash of that. The heat must be watched
and constantly adjusted. All could be
ruined at any moment: up in flames.
It's better to cook alone. Don't let
non-cooks stand around complimenting
you as you work. This is not helpful.
If they start to tell you how good things
smell, or how skilled you are, your head
may swell and your flame go out.
Only by being alone in the kitchen
can you let that touch of madness
that makes a cook's genius
have free rein. Mistakes along
the way, as Julia Child taught us,
need not be divulged to diners.
Some cooks like to collaborate.

I recommend caution. The end result
is often a failed marriage of techniques.
That is unless your fellow cook is so
attuned to your kitchen rhythms and
you to theirs that you can work together
as one, predicting and anticipating each
other, letting the food be your guide.
Before you bring your dish to table,
take a deep breath and, as the Irish
poet Yeats wrote, "cast a cold eye"
upon it. Is the meat properly cooked?
Have the garnishes been added?
How many plates have been rushed
to table out of hunger or excitement
while those gestures of last-minute polish,
a shower of pepper, a parsley cascade,
are neglected? Remember, in the end,
it is better to let food, as the Roman
poet Horace advised of manuscripts, rest.
Overly hot food will do no more than
scorch the taste buds, while a meal
that's presented at the perfect moment
will fill the soul with lasting nourishment.

# Druthers (3)

FOR JASON MITCHELL, ON HIS BIRTHDAY

I would rather listen to tercets
On Blind *Amor*, than defenses
Explaining what Poetry's good for.

I would rather the poem's score
My ear imprison, than enumerate
The wrongs of late capitalism.

# How Poets Came PhDs

AFTER HERRICK'S "HOW LILIES CAME WHITE"

Doctors though ye be; yet, Poets, know,
From the first ye were not so:
But I'll tell ye
What befell ye:
Far worse than Plato's banishment—
Which for dialectic's envy
Of your mimetic *topos*
Was ever took
(Knowing Sophia's *philos*
For reason's book
Could never quite capture
Your divine rapture)
—Has been modernity's frenzy
For naught but mere efficiency:
'Tis Econ 101
Which hath the poet undone

As well as our time's perverse conviction
  That things called "theoretical"
  Out-merit things poetical.
Ye makers, once masters of craft and line,
  Are now to *curriculum vitae*
  Beholden
And your Muse is Sick, nigh
  Moribund,
  And Plato's finally won.

# Birder

FOR ROBERT ADAMSON

Vouchsafe this poem to the one
in need of a falcon to wake him,
of songbirds to keep time's secret
stitched in syntax lace. Should
he be astonished that lepers vanish
in the wake of embraces, let
the footprints of God lead the way.
And if it happens that his father
sold cloth, he may disrobe and
be led by the neck with a rope
in an effort to denude his soul.
But since he's never been an ass,
let this not be so. Such crumbs
as are poems have fallen in line
before reaching his mouth.
Let his affections remind

those who are holy "just for show"
that Lady Poverty loves French poetry
more than pious sermons.
Forgiveness is in him, just
as form and matter are in bodies
married, in poems embraced.
In his company anger dissipates,
joy increases. From where did he
learn such gentle courtesy?
This cheerful measure
of meager fare? From a bit
of honest fear, and a fishing line
of gold; from a drop of crimson
at the point of each wound;
from work as an interpreter
of the gospel of the birds.

## These Houses

echo each other, corset
memory, they are temporal
nets, beginnings that end.
Clock face *à coté*,
radio wave, hot
running water:
all the conditions
for dream acquisition.
A postwar-childhood
home on the cheap,
open parenthesis
to presence, rambling
preamble to several
shabby unsettled
apartments, trash cans
catching the ceiling's
expression, where
the ragged *now*

governed in liberty, en route to

the *will be* and the *once was*,

or so it was thought

until those suspensions

became naught but middle,

nowhere to settle

in grammatical mind.

Because this house *is*,

it de-ambitions, its

darkness can lead me,

is as safe as can be.

In it the *once was*,

and *will be*

have left me. A closed

parenthesis escapes

the mind's files,

a coda to presence

which brings my

echo, that house

"once upon a time"

to bear, and rots it.

## Up to the Minute

The violence of the human world does not scale.
Digits thumb up the glow until the clip, the feed, the ad
Shoot through the eyes into the head. The backed-up
Neglected rooms shake with new poisons, information, and numbers.
The unfilmed quiet that follows the rifle. Heads: of state, severed,
In a mass, rivers of adrenaline compelled by violence,
Human, worldly, tearful or gleeful, all is turned to rage.

The old—never again will there be such as are now.
The wind knows what to do. The snow. The little life
That's lost beneath the Earth's benevolent death.
As we try to sleep the screened-in head ignites
With endless clips of violence. This is our truth?
What's muffled: some thought about hope
In an old book that somebody by candlelight
Wrote the moment she knew all hope was gone.

Crumpled youth can still laugh at death, but any age
Can apply this mortal urge to resignation, or righteousness
To create more bright violence. Here is belief?
Humans are lit up: we can know all and see everything,
Face the hatred and be mistaken for brave, raise our
Convulsive fist in an attempt to conform to new
Scales of violence reflected off these surfaces,
Distracting us from other worlds, inward, or yet begun.

## On Her Success

On the Poets' Registry of Graves
there may be listed an address,
the number of a humble plot
in some Mount Hope or Pleasant View.
But since marble is costly
they'll be no obelisk or angel
dressed in fancy stone for me.
Look for my name engraved
in black granite, lying flat against
the ground. Be careful, you might
pass by it, obscured by the lawn's
green stubble. Are you paying me
a visit because a poem of mine
once undid you, just a little?
Have you brought a flower?
Though dead, I'm hardly inured
to such gestures—the thoughtful
violence of something plucked.

If you plan to spend time, bring
a bottle of red, not California,
but French. Sit beside me and read
some Whitman. If you grow
woozy from the drink and heat,
all the better. Stretch out and look up.
Know—but wait, you must already—
that though in life I may have been
excluded from the highest echelons
of poetry, derelict in my courtship
of Lady Fortune, now from this
deep earth and from these lines,
and from any reverie they spark
in you, none can my spirit evict.

# Druthers (4)

I would rather have the dead's respect
Than all the laurels the living bestow,
A good hard cry swell up my eyes
Than a poetry prize my ego.

## The Spark

I wrote this happiness myself.
I chose this man, this house, this cat.
I put my shadow twin
upstairs in the leaf of a
mediocre book I thought
never to open again. I felt grateful.

Upstairs there were many
photo albums with gluey pages
and yellowed Mylar in between
which Polaroids had come
unstuck. In them happy children
pitch tents, watch TV,
open presents, and smile before
homemade birthday cakes.
Had I known them? I knew

that I was not missing them
or missing out and thus my heart
was full. But, I thought,
should phosphorus mix
with potassium chlorate
and hit the gaseous air,
this man, this house, this cat,
be lost, what then? They'd join
the many other dead
whose memories I tend.
I cannot miss. My heart is full

and grateful. But, I thought,
while I still could, should
neural plaques and tangles
knot my mind, my heart would
empty and all of this would
cease to be. I could not miss it,
nor even this, my spark.

# Acknowledgments

"And the Angels Sing" was written for *You Smile and the Angels Sing,* an artist's book by Alex Katz published by Lococo Fine Art Publisher in 2017. "Orbit Music" was recorded in August 2016 for the podcast *PoetryNow*, a partnership between the Poetry Foundation and the WFMT Radio Network. "The Bittersweet Echo" and "The Poetry Lesson" were included in *On Rhyme*, edited by David Caplan and published by the Presses Universitaires de Liège in 2017. "A *Bouquet Garni* for Rosmarie" was published in a Festschrift for Rosmarie Waldrop on her eightieth birthday, compiled by Ben Lerner and Anna Moschovakis and published by Ugly Duckling Presse in 2015. Thank you also to the editors of the following magazines where versions of some of these poems appeared: *Columbia Poetry Review, Company, The Hampden-Sydney Poetry Review,* and *Subtropics.*

JENNIFER MOXLEY IS A POET, ESSAYIST,
AND TRANSLATOR. SHE LIVES IN MAINE
WITH HER HUSBAND STEVE EVANS.